50 GAMES
TO PLAY WITH
YOUR CAT

JACKIE STRACHAN
foreword by Franny Syufy

IVY PRESS

This edition published in the UK in 2016 by

Ivy Press

210 High Street

Lewes

East Sussex BN7 2NS

United Kingdom

www.ivypress.co.uk

First published in the UK in 2007

British Library Cataloguing-in-Publication Data

A catalogue record for this book is available from the British Library

ISBN: 978-1-78240-353-1

This book was conceived, designed and produced by

Ivy Press

Creative Director Peter Bridgewater

Publisher Jason Hook

Editorial Director Caroline Earle

Senior Project Editor Stephanie Evans

Art Director Sarah Howerd

Project Designer Suzie Johanson

Designer Clare Barber

Illustrator Joanna Kerr

Photography Nick Ridley

This book has been published with the intent to provide accurate and
authoritative information in regard to the subject matter within. While every
reasonable precaution has been taken in preparation of this book, the author and
publisher expressly disclaim responsibility for any errors, omissions, or adverse
effects arising from the use or application of the information contained herein.
The techniques and suggestions are used at the reader's discretion and are not
to be considered a substitute for veterinary care. If you suspect a medical problem
consult your veterinarian.

Printed in China

10 9 8 7 6 5 4 3 2 1

Contents

Foreword

I've enjoyed the company of cats for several decades, and watching their antics at play has brought me countless hours of chuckles and laughter. While cats can be very serious at their games, their acrobatics and contortions are amusing to watch.

A kitten first learns to play from its mother. However, she does not consider it 'play' as such, but rather as teaching necessary survival skills, such as establishing territory, and the ever-present need to search for prey. This holds true, whether the cats are pampered house cats, fed in fancy dishes or stray alley cats. Their mother cats taught each one of them the art of stalking, pouncing and catching mice and other prey for their dinners.

The pet industry recognises these truths, and cat toys, climbing towers and scratching posts are designed to satisfy cats' innate survival needs. However, I learned by observation long ago that my cats were more likely to play inside the box their new toy came in than with the toy itself. While we may take satisfaction in the fact that we are willing to spend oodles of cash for our kitties' happiness and fun, the truth is that cats don't give a hoot about expense. They know what they enjoy, and it isn't necessarily a plush cat 'palace'.

A cat loves the delicious rustling noise a paper bag makes when he chases his tail inside it. He becomes a fanatic over batting at a 'bird' made from coloured felt or a ball of wool as it flies temptingly close to his eager claws. The creators of *50 Games to Play with Your Cat*

recognise cats' simple approach to play and exercise. They have designed ingenious and simple games, toys and accessories that you can easily create that will keep your cat happily occupied for hours.

If you are creatively inclined, you may want to make artistic 'improvements' on some of the creations herein, such as graffiti on the inside walls of the 'Escape to Alcatraz' cat clink (*see page 122*). Or maybe, a fair feline Rapunzel hanging out of the window of the elegant castle (*see page 26*). Or you can simply line up open-ended boxes for a cat tunnel. Your cat will enjoy one version every bit as much as the other. You'll likely find him curling up for a snooze in his jail cell after catching and killing that felt bird, or taking a 'cat nap' in the cat tunnel after a tough game of hide and seek enjoyed with another cat.

I particularly appreciated the fact that the book stresses the safety side of cat toys, and wish some of those commercial manufacturers would do the same. I've seen too much shoddy workmanship with small parts that break off cat toys and become a hazard. Cats are very serious about their play, and they really try to 'kill' those toy mice with a vengeance.

Are they having fun while they practise their life skills? They aren't talking, but I bet they are!

Franny Syufy
About.com Guide to Cats
http://cats.about.com

Introduction

Playing with your cat brings numerous benefits – as well as providing mental stimulation, the exercise will stretch muscles and tendons, improving circulation and muscle tone. Play also helps you to bond one-to-one with your cat, building trust and affection, and can act as therapy by giving a shy, retiring cat confidence or relieving the stress of a visit to the vet.

PLAYING BY THE RULES

To get the maximum benefit from your cat play, follow these top tips for feline fun:

- How often? Play two or three times a day, for 10–15 minutes at a time, or until he gets tired – you will soon know when he has had enough because he will either ignore you and stalk off, or ignore you and sit down to wash.
- When? Cats are often frisky early in the morning and also late at night, so 10 minutes of quality time before you start work and just before bed might help to promote restful sleep (both his and yours).

- Is your cat in the mood? If your cat is racing around, wild-eyed or is hopping about sideways, stiff-legged, he is feeling frisky and ready to play.

- Be a team player. Most cats will play alone, but will also appreciate playing with you. It is far more fun chasing a piece of string (pulled by you), or swiping at a feather (dangled by you) than prodding an inanimate toy masquerading as a mouse. Don't leave an indoor cat to his own devices all the time. It simply isn't fair to him.

- Is he having fun? If his pupils are dilated or he is purring he is having a good time. If he growls, squeals, whacks his tail on the floor or starts waving his claws around, it's time to stop the game.

- Don't be the parent who always has to win. Let him have the satisfaction of catching the feather, ball or wool sometimes or he will lose interest quickly.

- Keep toys fresh. Put them away at the end of each session and rotate them for interest. If you leave one or two out for solo play, never leave out pieces of string or wool which could be swallowed and cause great harm (*see page 10*).

- Is it different for kittens? Young cats and kittens are usually ready for a game, whereas older and more sedentary cats will want to play less often.

- How to stop? If you want to end the session, wind down the play in order not to leave him in an excited state, gradually applying less movement to a toy so that it 'dies', just like prey in the wild.

Safety First

Making playtime safe for your cat is mostly a matter of common sense, and you should carefully check toys and games in the same way that you would for a small child, applying the same criteria. However, there are a few extra points to be aware of that apply specifically to cats.

CURIOSITY COULD KILL A CAT

Be extremely vigilant when your cat is playing with wool, cord, string, etc., basically anything that is long, thin and dangles enticingly. Never allow your cat to play unsupervised with toys that are attached to string or cord, as it could get caught around her neck or paws and strangle or hurt her. If a cat gets caught, her natural reaction is to struggle, which could make things worse, causing the string to tighten or cut into the flesh.

Most cats are pretty sensible, but some seem to have a mental block when it comes to string or wool and love to swallow it. They don't even chew it off into manageable pieces, but can swallow metres of it. String or wool can cause great harm if it reaches the intestines, and it could be fatal. If you know your cat has swallowed some, or you see any protruding from her mouth or rectum, never attempt to pull it out. Instead, cut it off close to the cat and take her to the vet immediately.

You must therefore never leave your cat to play alone with wool, ribbon, beads or anything similar, and it is important to keep household items such as string or dental floss put away.

Check your home for other potential attractions, such as the cords from curtains or blinds and electrical wires – especially if your cat likes to chew them.

Check too for any sharp protrusions that could also cause harm. Keep an eye on all toys and replace them once they begin to show signs of wear and tear.

OTHER THINGS TO WATCH:

- Make sure soft toys are washable so that you can keep them clean, and check to make sure that the filling is not likely to come out. If it is, throw away that toy!
- Always cut the handles off shopping and carrier bags. Your cat could easily get her neck caught in one.
- Never leave plastic bags lying around. In the same way that these are a hazard for children, your cat could creep into one and suffocate.
- Do not leave small pieces of plastic lying around as some cats like to chew and swallow it. They are also attracted to anything shiny or crackly, so stay on hand for any impromptu play with aluminium foil or bubble wrap.
- If you are making a toy for your cat, always make sure you use non-toxic materials in case your cat licks or chews part of it, and avoid adding small details such as whiskers, which could be pulled off and swallowed.

CATNIP AND HOUSEPLANTS

Cats cannot become addicted to catnip, but some could become overstimulated and even aggressive. Use it sparingly. Also, be aware that some houseplants are toxic to cats – read their advice labels for warnings.

PLAY SAFE

Never allow your cat to play with items such as rubber bands, ring-pulls from cans, Christmas tinsel, paper clips, pins and drawing pins or perished balloons, etc. Be on the alert for anything small that your cat might like to play with: far better to be safe than sorry.

On the Prowl

Cats are natural-born skilled hunters and there's nothing they like better than to stalk and chase. You can channel all that feline instinct and energy by ensuring your cat has the sort of activities that enable him to display his hunting prowess, but without harming any small furred or feathered friends in the great outdoors. This way, everybody wins.

Simple Toys

One of the great things about being a cat owner is that you don't need to spend a lot of money to keep him entertained. If you want to buy an elaborate cat tree or a special cat toy, there are some truly fantastic and fun items available, but your cat will probably equally enjoy playing with toys that cost very little – or nothing. In fact, you can come up with all kinds of toys in just a few seconds using everyday objects that you find around the home.

▼ BELOW Even the most simple material that your cat plays with needs to be strong and well made to stand up to rough treatment from his teeth and claws.

▶ RIGHT Most cats enjoy taking a swipe at a dangling toy and you don't have to buy anything readymade – improvise with a cork on a piece of string.

FUN FROM EVERYDAY OBJECTS

Small, light objects made of wood or plastic, such as shower curtain rings or drinking straws bent into shapes, make cat-friendly toys. Cats often find their own toys, playing with small things that have dropped to the floor. Always ensure a new 'toy' is safe for him.

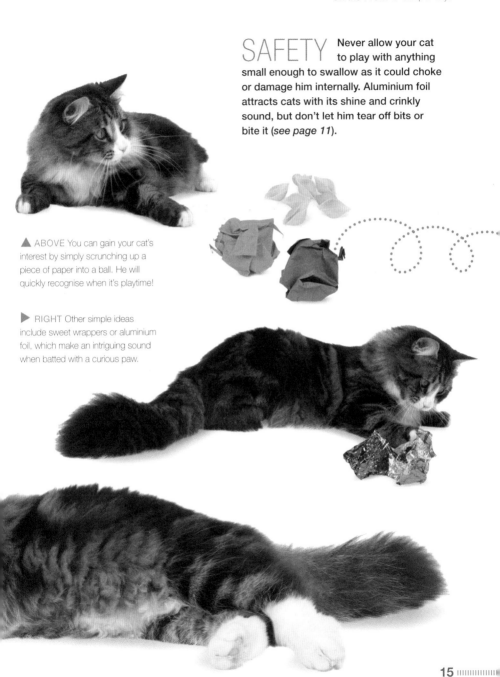

SAFETY
Never allow your cat to play with anything small enough to swallow as it could choke or damage him internally. Aluminium foil attracts cats with its shine and crinkly sound, but don't let him tear off bits or bite it (*see page 11*).

▲ ABOVE You can gain your cat's interest by simply scrunching up a piece of paper into a ball. He will quickly recognise when it's playtime!

▶ RIGHT Other simple ideas include sweet wrappers or aluminium foil, which make an intriguing sound when batted with a curious paw.

15

IN A SPIN

Many other household objects can double up as toys – almost anything small that rolls, from a spool reel to the cork from a bottle. When batted at one end, small plastic bottles or containers will also spin around, adding to the fun.

On a Roll

▲ ABOVE Got it! But probably not for long – balls have a habit of rolling out of reach, so your cat will get plenty of exercise from stretching for them as well as chasing after them (and so will you as you retrieve them from under the sofa, bed or fridge).

Small balls and other round objects also make great toys. With one tap of a paw, they shoot and skitter across the floor at speed while your cat gives chase. Ping-pong balls are the perfect size and are also light enough for your cat to bat easily. Standard golf balls are a little too heavy to bat across some surfaces, but small plastic practice golf balls with holes in them are great. Claws can be hooked into the holes for a bit of juggling and your cat might get a hole in one – Tiger Woods beware!

◀ LEFT You won't need to look far around your home to find fun cat toys, just make sure they are clean and safe in the event of any experimental biting.

▼ BELOW The game becomes more interesting if you roll the toy under a chair, or behind the curtains. Make it hard to get and your intrepid hunter will enjoy the fun even more.

▼ BELOW Don't always be too quick to retrieve the object: your cat will enjoy possessing his prize and will continue to play on his own.

Hot Pursuit

Cats love the thrill of the chase, so a simple game with either a nicely tactile 'mouse' made from fabric or string to get to grips with or, for more energetic action, a wind-up version, is usually an instant winner. Of course, once you've set them off, wind-up toys race around under their own steam. Some move in a satisfyingly erratic way, changing direction suddenly, just like real prey. If you want the upmarket equivalent, there are even remote-control mouse lookalikes on the market, which can provide great entertainment and exercise.

▲ ABOVE Cats will often seem to 'encourage' a toy mouse to move, just so that they can pounce and continue the game.

◀ LEFT Intent on his prey, tail and whiskers quivering, your cat's fur-lined claws are ready to make a lightning strike.

▼ BELOW A self-propelled mouse might elude your cat with its erratic path, but only for so long!

CATCH ME IF YOU CAN

||||||||||||||||||||||||||||||||||||||||||||||||||||||||||||||||||||||||||||||||||||||||||||||||||||||||||

You can mimic the action of a real mouse by making a wind-up version run along a skirting board. Put a small open cardboard box against a wall so that the 'mouse' can dash for its hole, with your cat in hot pursuit. Cut away the side of the box that lies on the floor so there is no lip to stop the toy entering the box.

▼ BELOW After an exciting chase, your cat will want his reward … stay on hand to make sure whatever he chews is not going to come apart and be swallowed.

Pompom Play

Cats love playing with pompoms worked up in soft wool, which become all the more irresistible if they are dangling on a string. You can easily make the pompoms yourself, using up odd bits of wool, in the old-fashioned way. It's a good idea to make several pompoms at once as you might find your cat's favourite game is pulling them to pieces. Cats like to grasp the pompom with their front paws and claws and bury their faces in the soft, warm wool. They will sometimes want to tug with their teeth at the strands of wool, pulling bits out, so make sure you tie the centre of the pompom as tightly as possible with a strong piece of wool (*see Box opposite*) and stay to watch the fun in case the play gets rough.

▲ ABOVE Pompom purrah! You and your cat can get creative in this game involving some precision cheerleader moves.

SAFETY Stay with your cat at all times because your pompom is likely to be in for some rough play. Remove any bits of wool that are pulled out and on no account allow your cat to chew or swallow the wool. Put away the pompoms when the game is over.

▲ ABOVE The combination of soft woolly pompom and dangling string is usually just too much to resist.

▲◄ ABOVE AND LEFT
Remove the pompoms if your cat shows signs of getting bored and in order not to risk diminishing his responsiveness for next time.

HOW TO MAKE POMPOMS

|||||||||||||||||||||||||||||||||||||||||||||||||||||||||||||||||||||||||||||||||||||

Cut out two 'doughnuts' from thin card. Hold the disks together and wind wool tightly around them. You can add other colours as you go. Continue winding until the hole is tightly filled and tie off the ends of the wool. Cut the wool between the two disks with scissors. Wind a length of wool several times around the centre, tie tightly, then ease off the card disks.

▲ ABOVE Initially, engage your cat by making the smallest sound or movement with the toy on a string.

▲ ABOVE Once he's interested, let him creep up on the prey for a while before making it retreat.

The Thing on a String

Have you ever been winding up a ball of string or wool to find it has snagged on something below? You look down to find that the 'something' is a small furry paw. Unable to resist anything that dangles or slithers, your cat has just had to pounce. The Thing on a String is a classic homemade toy that's super-easy to make. Ideal things to tie to the end of your string include a favourite toy, a piece of scrunched-up paper, a feather, a cork, a pompom ... Or the string can even be left bare, with just a few knots tied at the end to enable your cat to get a better grip with his claws and teeth.

▼ BELOW The 'Thing' on the string can take many forms – scrunched-up paper, a cork, or simply a knot at the end.

SAFETY

Few cats can resist a piece of string or wool, with or without a toy attached, but you should never leave your cat to play unsupervised with string, wool or anything similar. Some cats like to swallow it, which could do them great harm (*see page 10*).

▼ BELOW Hooked!

▼ BELOW Allow your cat his fun but be vigilant, and never pull the string tight as it could catch in his teeth or claws, or wrap around a paw and hurt him.

Feathered Friends

It's hardly surprising that most cats like playing with feathers, since it's the next best thing to stalking a real bird. Your cat can have fun without affecting the local bird population. Try holding a large feather behind the furniture so that just the tip is visible and watch her stalk it.

Feathers flutter enticingly, so your cat might enjoy playing if you position her toy where it will catch a breeze. Tie several feathers to a short piece of string attached to a wand and secure it to a flat surface such as the floor or a low table, or, if you have a garden, simply stick it in the ground.

▲ ABOVE Dangle feathers just above and in front of your cat or pull one slowly across the floor for her to chase.

◀ LEFT Peacock feathers are a great choice because the quills are so long. You can keep your hands well out of the way of those claws, and jiggle the end.

▶ RIGHT You can buy a mini boa specially made for cats which can be stalked, chased and generally roughed up – almost like a feathered snake!

SAFETY It's important that you only allow your cat to play with feathers when supervised. Cats love to eat them, and the sharp quills can result in internal harm. Be careful with larger feathers as the edges can cause damage to your cat's eyes if they are accidentally hit or poked during a game.

HOW TO MAKE A FEATHERED FRIEND

Draw bird and wing outlines on paper as templates.
Cut two bird and two wing shapes out of felt. Stitch the
curved end of each wing to each bird shape. Place the
bird shapes wrong sides together and stitch the edges,
leaving a small gap. Insert cat-friendly synthetic filling
through the gap and stitch it up. Stitch a small feather
behind each wing, and attach to string.

▲ ABOVE You can dangle the
bird enticingly in front of your cat,
or attach it to a chair (or even a
houseplant) for your cat to play with.
Stay on hand to watch the fun.

Peeping Tom

In days of old, when mice were bold and cats were in charge of rodent removal throughout the land, from humble hovel to princely palace, their role as pest control operatives kept them busy and in shape. These days, our pampered pets no longer need to earn their living or fend for themselves but they still enjoy a little medieval mayhem. Place a toy mouse or two inside the castle and let battle commence.

▼ BELOW Engage your cat's interest by placing a favourite toy where he can see it. Most cats love boxes and will need little encouragement to embark on a stakeout.

▼ BELOW Your cat's castle needs to be sturdy enough to withstand a little paw pressure and even the odd full-scale assault.

SAFETY It's a good idea to secure the 'castle' to the floor with tape to prevent it from sliding around or getting knocked over should the action turn boisterous. As well as ensuring a sturdy construction, check that the top of the castle doesn't have sharp edges in case an approach from the battlements ends in a crash landing.

HOW TO GET THE FORTIFIED EFFECT

If you want your castle to look really convincing you can buy stone-effect paper made for doll's house enthusiasts which gives the correct proportions. A castellated top to the walls completes the effect. Have your main 'gate' large enough for him to get a good view inside, with paw-sized arches for him to make a grab for that speeding mouse.

▲ ABOVE Your cat will stay alert by the hole, anticipating the slightest move or sound. You can attach the mouse to a string and give little tugs to make it appear to run.

▼ BELOW Got it! All that patient watching and waiting is rewarded in the end.

Invisible Mouse

This is a great game for sharpening the reflexes – yours as well as your cat's if you are feeling brave and play with your finger. Depending on its thickness, the material concealing the 'mouse' should save your skin to some extent, although the needle-sharp claws of an excited cat could still draw blood through thin fabric. Otherwise, a pen or pencil will do just as well. Wiggle the pen beneath the cover to emulate darting, mouse-like movements – watch your cat's reaction and be prepared for the lightning-quick pounce.

BEDBUG

||||||||||||||||||||||||||||||||||||||||||||||||||||||||||||||||||||||||||||||||||||||||||||||||||||||||||

Many cats invent their own version of Invisible Mouse, as you'll know if you have ever had your toes attacked on a lazy Sunday morning in bed. So make the most of your cat's lively mood to play Bedbug beneath the sheets, but use a tightly rolled sock or a toothbrush. Exercise care as always, or vulnerable fingers and toes could still be mistaken for Sunday brunch.

▼ BELOW If your cat can spot your fingers, it's probably time to take your hand away!

▼ BELOW Once her attention is fully on the game, your cat will probably continue to go after her invisible prey well after you have removed your hand.

Cat Confidential

Just what is it with cats and paper? No cat seems able to resist a piece of paper placed on the floor – whether you are trying to wrap a gift or catch up on the news, your cat will soon be sitting smugly in the centre of it. Take advantage of this strange compulsion to play Cat Confidential, but only use paper that you no longer need – Great-Uncle Arthur's will or your favourite glossy magazine will soon get torn to shreds when play becomes boisterous.

▶ RIGHT Buy or sell? Your cat is not really checking on her investment in Purry Meat Chunks, she just loves the crinkly sound made by newspaper.

THIS TAKES TWO

Make the game more interesting by moving a pencil around or pulling along a piece of string under the paper: your cat will just have to pounce. Or, with your cat sitting on it, take hold of a corner of the paper and pull it slowly or in short jerks. She will either attack it with gusto or simply enjoy the ride.

◀ LEFT Try gently pulling a piece of string under the paper – your cat will find it impossible to sit still.

▶ RIGHT Make scratching sounds under the paper with your fingernail, but be ready to pull your hand away quickly just before she pounces.

◀ LEFT Allow your cat to check out the glove with claws and paws early on in the game, so he knows just what he is dealing with.

▼ BELOW Dangle the glove just above your cat's head and he'll soon be taking a swipe at those inviting 'fingers'.

▲ ABOVE If your cat is confused by having so many fingers to choose from, make it easy for him and use your forefinger only, tucking your remaining fingers into your palm.

Fingers of Fun

Using your bare hand to play with your cat could soon end in tears and they won't be your cat's! He cannot be expected to tell the difference between your fingers and a toy mouse when both are peeping out at him invitingly from beneath a cushion. Your yelp as you snatch your hand away will only leave him feeling bewildered and possibly frightened, or make him stalk off. Wearing a specially designed glove to play with your cat will fix the problem. Its extra-long fingers mean that yours remain safely out of reach.

SAFETY Cats of a very nervous disposition could find the long fingers intimidating if you forget the formalities and don't introduce the glove gently to them first. The 'fingers' are reinforced with wire or plastic so do make sure there are no sharp points protruding through the fabric that could hurt your cat.

▲ ABOVE Are you feeling sleepy? Hypnotised by the glove? Don't be fooled. He's just about to take a well-aimed swipe.

▶ RIGHT Always allow your cat the satisfaction of the occasional 'kill'. It's no problem with this game that takes the 'Hey!' out of play.

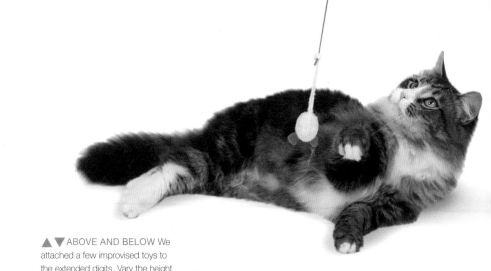

▲ ▼ ABOVE AND BELOW We
attached a few improvised toys to
the extended digits. Vary the height
at which your cat can play by tying
toys to the end of a piece of string.

Footloose

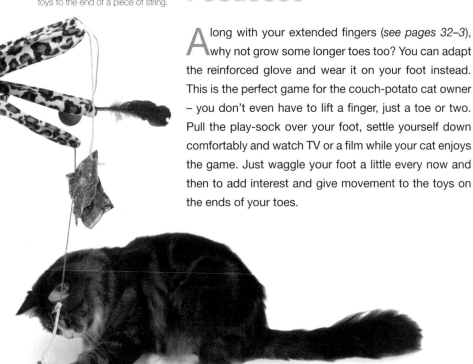

Along with your extended fingers (*see pages 32–3*), why not grow some longer toes too? You can adapt the reinforced glove and wear it on your foot instead. This is the perfect game for the couch-potato cat owner – you don't even have to lift a finger, just a toe or two. Pull the play-sock over your foot, settle yourself down comfortably and watch TV or a film while your cat enjoys the game. Just waggle your foot a little every now and then to add interest and give movement to the toys on the ends of your toes.

▶ RIGHT Attach small light-weight, cat-friendly toys to the end of each 'toe', such as a ball, a cork or a feather – even a scrunched-up sweet wrapper.

SAFETY Don't hold your foot so high that your cat becomes over-excited and twists and jumps too energetically. Resting your foot on a low stool or box will make it easier for both of you to sustain the fun. *See page 33 for other safety points relating to this game.*

▲ ABOVE Paper toys make an intriguing rustle when tapped, while wooden items can be made to bounce unpredictably off the chair legs, extending your cat's interest.

Cativity

This cats-only version of a baby's activity mat draws inspiration from a children's nursery. All you need are a number of small toys attached securely to lengths of string, ribbon or wool. Tie the toys to something solid that won't tip over – a heavy chair is good – and your cat will have lots to choose from. Suspend the toys at different heights to give him scope to play sitting or lying on his side. You can use a variety of toys and small cat-friendly objects from around the home.

SAFETY

At the end of play, put away toys that you would not want your cat to play with while you are not present. If you decide to leave any out, make sure they are safely attached to the string or wool and that this in turn is safely attached to the support. Some cats like to swallow string, which is extremely harmful (*see page 10*).

▶ RIGHT Don't use your best furniture for this game, just in case your cat decides to sharpen his claws when he's finished playing.

CAT MOBILE

||||||||||||||||||||||||||||||||||||||||||||||||||||||||||||||||||||||||||||||||||||||||||

You can also make a simple mobile by hanging toys from two horizontal slats of wood, joined in a cross at the centre. Or you can rig up a more elaborate one suspended from the top of a door or window frame. The slightest breeze will cause the objects to sway, instantly attracting your cat's attention. For glow-in-the-dark fun, you might include small balls that flash, or fluorescent plastic toys, tied on securely.

◀ LEFT Anything within reach becomes fair game, so vary the height of the suspended toys to sustain your cat's interest.

Feline Groovy

Cats are slaves to sensation and if there's one thing that hits the spot for most cats pleasure-wise, apart from snoozing in their favourite seat in front of the fire, it's catmint, or catnip. There are plenty of toys to buy that already contain catnip, but you can also add it yourself to make existing toys and games more fun. But don't worry if your feline seems to enjoy catnip just a little too much – it is non-addictive and completely legal!

Catnip Crazy

How do you make a silk purse out of a sow's ear in cat terms? For most of our feline friends, catnip has the power to turn even the saddest, most boring, and ragged inanimate toy mouse into something deeply fascinating. If your cat has turned his back on that all-singing, all-dancing toy that you bought at great expense, use catnip to make it more interesting. There are plenty of toys already stuffed with catnip to buy in the shops – but you can easily make your own too. Catnip comes in dried, powder and spray forms, but you can also grow your own and use it fresh. Despite its euphoric effect, the herb catmint (*Nepeta cataria*) is perfectly safe and it's not addictive. Grow it in your garden or in pots in full sun, but make sure you choose one of the scented varieties as some are purely ornamental.

▲ ABOVE Fresh catmint (bruise the leaves slightly) and the dried version, shown here, are the most effective forms but you can also buy it in a concentrated spray and as powder.

▼ BELOW Catnip should make the game more exciting – though it can turn some cats aggressive. This catnip-filled snake stands no chance!

▼ BELOW Now the prey has been overpowered, your cat can settle down and enjoy the catnip sensation.

▼ BELOW Your cat will play with his toy on his own quite happily until the effect of the catnip begins to wear off.

▲ ABOVE Striped, slinky, slithery … a little catnip can make even the most unlikely of toys look attractive.

RUSTLESNAKE!

This striped snake was quickly made using a pair of child's tights, stuffed and tied in sections, which means the snake can adopt some very lifelike positions! The body segments are padded with more of the striped fabric and contain cellophane sweet wrappers as well as catnip. This means the snake rustles – if not rattles – when 'attacked' by your cat.

Love in a Glove

Here's another great toy that is really simple to make. Sprinkle some straw or raffia with catnip powder or spray, pack it into an old woollen or fabric glove and tie up the end securely with strong wool or twine. You need to push the filling in quite tightly in case play becomes rough. If you find the catnip falls out before you can pack the filling into the glove, try sprinkling catnip into the empty glove first and then adding the filling. If the glove starts to lose its appeal for your cat, you probably just need to renew the catnip. Untie the end of the glove, remove the filling, shake out the old catnip, and replace with new.

▼ BELOW Show the filled glove to your cat and allow her to become aware of the catnip it contains. She'll soon get up close and personal, grasping it between her front paws and rubbing her cheek along it.

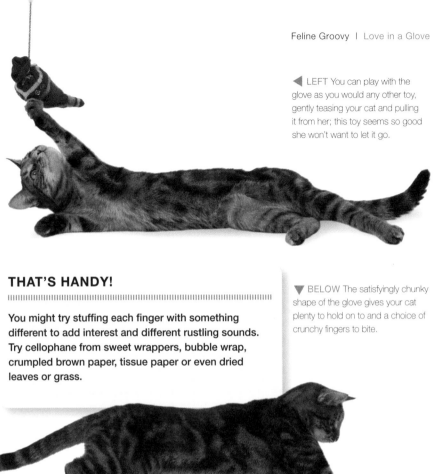

◀ LEFT You can play with the glove as you would any other toy, gently teasing your cat and pulling it from her; this toy seems so good she won't want to let it go.

THAT'S HANDY!

You might try stuffing each finger with something different to add interest and different rustling sounds. Try cellophane from sweet wrappers, bubble wrap, crumpled brown paper, tissue paper or even dried leaves or grass.

▼ BELOW The satisfyingly chunky shape of the glove gives your cat plenty to hold on to and a choice of crunchy fingers to bite.

SAFETY Catnip can unleash the inner tiger in some otherwise placid cats, making them more aggressive. Use with caution or not at all if it has this effect on your cat. It can also stimulate the appetite, a point to watch out for if your cat is already a little chunky.

▶ RIGHT A catnip pillow is another great way to keep your cat occupied. You won't need to include any toys, she will be stimulated enough by the scent.

Sweet Dreams

You would think that dreams on a pillow filled with catnip would be of the sweetest kind, but in reality the herby scent stimulates cats far too much to allow them to sleep. This game is very easy to set up – you simply need an old pillow or cushion. Sprinkle the catnip on the pillow, or, if you are worried about making a mess, put it inside between the cover and the filling. Padded mats filled with catnip are available commercially, but these are also easy to make at home and you can refill them when the scent wears off. The padding ensures that your cat has a soft surface to roll around on and rub up against. The stuff of feline dreams!

▼ BELOW The instinctive reaction of catnip-sensitive cats is to rub their cheeks over the catnip or the scented area.

SCENTS AND SENSIBILITY

||||||||||||||||||||||||||||||||||||||||||||||||||||||||||||||||||||||||||||||||||||||||||||||||||||||||||||||

Catnip doesn't do it for every cat – genetics and environment are believed to play a part in determining the level of responsiveness, with males tending to react more than females. The degree of response also varies, from a fairly mild rubbing of the cheeks against the catnip to frankly embarrassing displays of drooling and sheer ecstasy.

▲ ABOVE Kneading with the front paws is another very common feline reaction to catnip. Don't use your favourite pillowcase because it will end up more like a pincushion!

▲ ABOVE Tune in, turn on and roll about: sheer bliss! The effect can last anything from a few minutes to half an hour.

45

▲ ABOVE Yep. It smells just as good this way up too. With catnip around, the air will soon be filled with the sound of soft purring.

Pot Purry

A feline take on a fragrant pot-pourri for the home, this toy should ensure much pleasure and purring. You can purchase small plastic balls that come ready packaged with a little pouch of catnip in the centre. The smell of the catnip attracts your cat and holds her interest, while the rolling action of the ball itself will ensure she gets plenty of exercise as she chases it or jumps about. Choose those balls that can be opened in the centre, so that you can replenish the catnip from time to time. The ball itself is safe for your cat to play with solo, but if you attach it to string or ribbon, you should always stay present to join in the fun.

▼ BELOW To prevent loose catnip falling out of balls with larger holes, make your own pouch by wrapping some catnip in a square of thin cotton, tied tightly at the top.

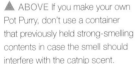

▲ ABOVE Putting catnip inside a ball means your cat has the added benefit of plenty of exercise as she chases it about.

▲ ABOVE If you make your own Pot Purry, don't use a container that previously held strong-smelling contents in case the smell should interfere with the catnip scent.

HOMEMADE HAPPINESS

It's easy enough to make your own scented ball. Make a number of holes in a small hollow ball using a skewer or knitting needle and poke some catnip inside. Alternatively, use a small container such as a plastic bottle with a cap and place the catnip inside. The holes should be numerous and large enough to allow the catnip odour to escape but not to let the catnip itself fall out easily, or you will have a messy trail to clean up.

Gone Fishin'

From cartoon cats throwing fish bones over their shoulders to fish-flavoured cat food and treats, everyone knows that cats love fish. And even if your cat shows a marked preference for food that once had limbs rather than fins, she may still like to indulge in a little fishing. Happily for you, this kind of fishing can be done from the comfort of your chair. All you need is a rod and line and for your cat to be in play mode. For simple, Huck Finn-style fishing, just attach a length of string to the end of a stick and tie on your bait. Your cat won't want to let this one get away, especially if you liven it up with some catnip!

▼ BELOW Show the fish to your cat and allow her to smell it, particularly if you have baited it with a little catnip.

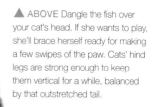

▲ ABOVE Dangle the fish over your cat's head. If she wants to play, she'll brace herself ready for making a few swipes of the paw. Cats' hind legs are strong enough to keep them vertical for a while, balanced by that outstretched tail.

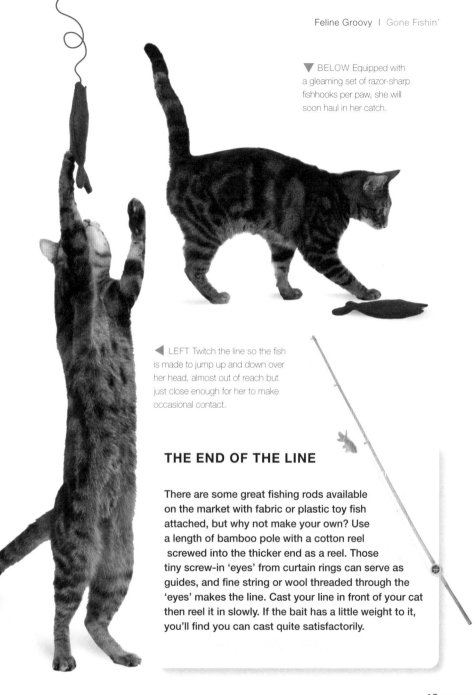

▼ BELOW Equipped with a gleaming set of razor-sharp fishhooks per paw, she will soon haul in her catch.

◀ LEFT Twitch the line so the fish is made to jump up and down over her head, almost out of reach but just close enough for her to make occasional contact.

THE END OF THE LINE

There are some great fishing rods available on the market with fabric or plastic toy fish attached, but why not make your own? Use a length of bamboo pole with a cotton reel screwed into the thicker end as a reel. Those tiny screw-in 'eyes' from curtain rings can serve as guides, and fine string or wool threaded through the 'eyes' makes the line. Cast your line in front of your cat then reel it in slowly. If the bait has a little weight to it, you'll find you can cast quite satisfactorily.

Tunnel Vision

When unsure, explore with a paw! Just what is in this interesting hole? This game makes the most of your cat's pathological need to squeeze an exploratory front paw into the most inaccessible of nooks and crannies, just in case some small hapless creature is hiding from him. Glue several cardboard tubes together in a sturdy shape, such as a pyramid or a log cabin, which will stand steady on a flat surface. Scrunch up some tissue paper loosely and sprinkle it generously with catnip. Push the tissue paper into a couple of the tubes for your cat to prise out with paw and claw.

▲ ABOVE With his nosy nature, your cat will be intrigued by all the interesting small spaces to explore and the scent of the catnip will only add to the fun.

▼ BELOW Don't use tubes that are too wide. They should be a perfect paw fit, just wide enough to enable your cat to reach inside and hook out the contents.

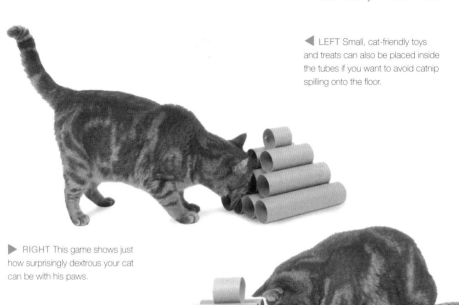

◀ LEFT Small, cat-friendly toys and treats can also be placed inside the tubes if you want to avoid catnip spilling onto the floor.

▶ RIGHT This game shows just how surprisingly dextrous your cat can be with his paws.

▼ BELOW Tunnel Vision is quite safe for your cat to play alone – provided you do not leave any small toys in the tubes that could form a choking hazard.

DRYING & STORING CATNIP

Hang a bunch of freshly cut catmint somewhere warm and dry. When it is completely dry, crumble the leaves into a bag, discarding any bits of stalk. To keep dried catnip as scented as possible, store it in a plastic bag in the freezer, or in an airtight tin or ceramic container in a cool, dry place. Protect the catnip from the light as UV rays will make it deteriorate more quickly.

What's In It for Me?

Games that make use of treats are perfect for cats who need a little incentive to get them into a playful frame of mind. Admittedly, there is an element of bribery involved but, used sensibly, treats can be your secret weapon in persuading more sedentary cats to join in the fun, and will also help encourage shy cats out of their shell (or from under the sofa). Just remember to use treats sparingly if your cat tends to be a little on the plump side.

It's All in the Packaging

There's nothing like a few boxes, bags and tubes to bring out the snoop in the average cat. By hiding a few cat treats in a selection of containers, you can make exploring them really worthwhile. Make it even more interesting by making the treats harder to get. For instance, place one beneath a piece of paper at the bottom of a box, or beneath some scrunched-up tissue paper in the compartment of an egg carton, squeeze one between two pieces of cardboard at the side of a box, or use a container that is partially closed or has a small opening, such as a disposable tissue box – so that he really has to work at getting them.

▼ BELOW Boxes, bags and tubes are all worthy of investigation, and you can place toys or treats in certain hidey-holes for extra fun.

◀ LEFT Perfect cat-friendly material. Cardboard boxes and egg cartons can be clawed, gnawed and generally treated roughly without any problem.

▶ RIGHT Those cats who have any tomboy tendencies will appreciate having a cardboard tube partially unwound so that they can finish the job and pull it apart.

SAFETY Make sure you use cat-friendly items only. Never use plastic bags and always cut the handles off paper bags – an inquisitive cat intent on exploring could easily get his head caught in them, causing distress and possible harm. Also check cardboard and containers for any sharp points that could hurt your cat, such as staples.

Cat Nav

Few can resist the lure of buried treasure and cats are no exception, though their idea of 'treasure' is a little different from ours. They might turn their noses up at precious jewels and gold doubloons but cat treats are another matter. Outside, the world is so full of different smells that your cat's sensitive nose is in action constantly. An outdoor treasure hunt is therefore best set up away from any overpowering smells and within a relatively small, safely enclosed area. Hide the treats in long grass, behind a flower pot or tucked between a few logs. If your cat is too distracted and you need to give his navigational skills some encouragement, try laying two or three treats in a trail to the treasure. If your cat is indoors only, try this game in a basement or garage.

▲ ABOVE Provided it is safe to do so, make use of whatever is to hand in the garden. Try tucking a treat behind or inside pots and containers.

◀ LEFT AND ABOVE If your cat is unsure how to play Cat Nav, show him a treat, allow him to smell it, and then let him watch you hiding it.

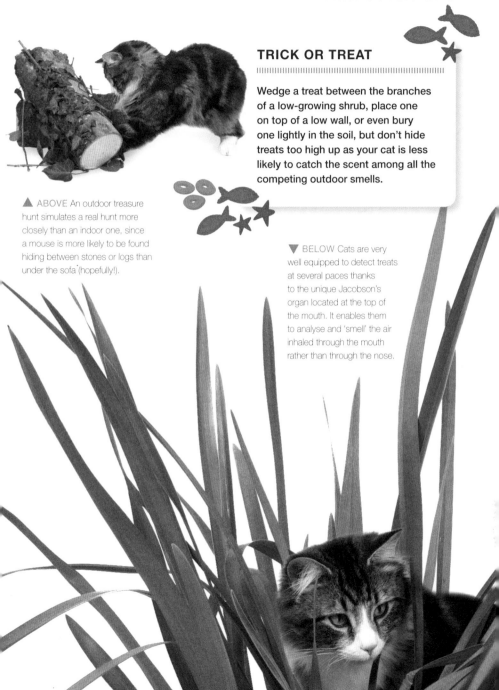

TRICK OR TREAT

Wedge a treat between the branches of a low-growing shrub, place one on top of a low wall, or even bury one lightly in the soil, but don't hide treats too high up as your cat is less likely to catch the scent among all the competing outdoor smells.

▲ ABOVE An outdoor treasure hunt simulates a real hunt more closely than an indoor one, since a mouse is more likely to be found hiding between stones or logs than under the sofa (hopefully!).

▼ BELOW Cats are very well equipped to detect treats at several paces thanks to the unique Jacobson's organ located at the top of the mouth. It enables them to analyse and 'smell' the air inhaled through the mouth rather than through the nose.

Inside Knowledge

Your cat knows every inch of her home intimately. She has explored behind every chair, every set of curtains and under every bed with her super-sensitive feline nose. It holds no surprises for her ... or does it? This treasure hunt will have her exploring her familiar surroundings all over again. Hide several of her favourite treats around the room. She should soon track them down, but if she doesn't, help her out by laying a trail. With your cat out of the room, draw a treat across the floor leaving a scent trail to its hiding place. Then bring her into the room, sit back and watch a consummate huntress at work.

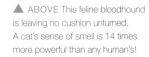

▲ ABOVE This feline bloodhound is leaving no cushion unturned. A cat's sense of smell is 14 times more powerful than any human's!

 LEFT Hiding treats in interesting places gives an added dimension to an otherwise familiar room.

▲ ABOVE The harder it is to find the treat, the more she has to use her ingenuity to win it. But don't make it impossible for her, and only hide things in safe places – not too high and never behind one of your precious ornaments.

TEST YOUR CAT'S 'SMELL IQ'

Cats rely very heavily on their sense of smell as their eyes cannot focus well close up. They use their noses to seek out edible food as well as to make sure it is the correct temperature. Test your cat's 'smell IQ' by placing a treat with a few other strongly smelling items, such as a piece of citrus peel, placed a few centimetres apart beneath some kitchen paper and see whether she heads for the treat immediately.

▲ ABOVE When your cat loses interest, the ball is almost certainly out of treats! For cats with a tendency to put on weight, it's best to restrict this game for special occasions only.

▲ ABOVE Your cat will soon realise that when she nudges the ball around with her nose something tasty will fall out.

Treats on Tap

▼ BELOW This is a purchased treat-dispenser, but you can easily make your own (*see Box opposite*).

All cats know where it's at when it comes to seeking out tasty morsels and fishy-flavoured goodies, so this game, which is played with a treat-dispensing ball, is bound to be a sure-fire winner. Place several of your cat's favourite treats (we used dried prawn) inside the ball and roll it towards her. She will soon detect the tantalising smell of the treats wafting out of the holes in the ball. As she bats the ball and rolls it around, the treats will fall out of the largest hole, one by one. With the treats as an incentive, she will soon catch on and chase the ball around to earn her edible rewards.

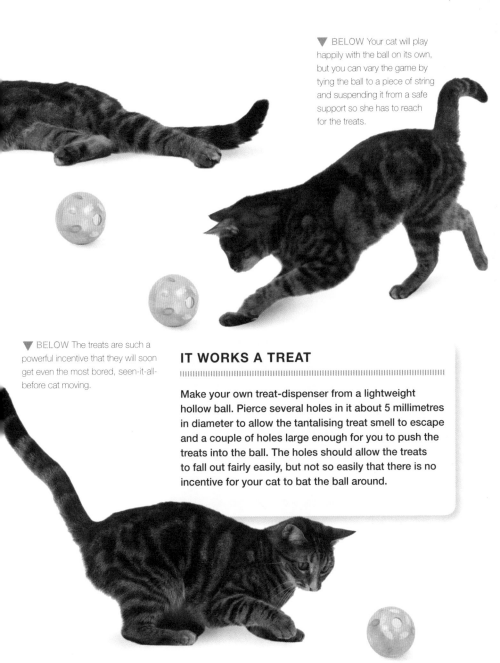

▼ BELOW Your cat will play happily with the ball on its own, but you can vary the game by tying the ball to a piece of string and suspending it from a safe support so she has to reach for the treats.

▼ BELOW The treats are such a powerful incentive that they will soon get even the most bored, seen-it-all-before cat moving.

IT WORKS A TREAT

Make your own treat-dispenser from a lightweight hollow ball. Pierce several holes in it about 5 millimetres in diameter to allow the tantalising treat smell to escape and a couple of holes large enough for you to push the treats into the ball. The holes should allow the treats to fall out fairly easily, but not so easily that there is no incentive for your cat to bat the ball around.

▼ BELOW In normal circumstances your cat would either ignore the calendar or at best choose it as a spot for a quick nap, but the smell of treats will attract her attention instantly.

▼ BELOW A cat's paws have very sensitive touch receptors that help them to explore the shape, size and texture of objects.

Catvent Calendar

You don't have to wait for the holiday season to play this countdown game – every day can be Christmas Day for your cat. Place a treat behind each of the doors and open one a day. Help your cat by prising the chosen door open slightly first, but the rest of the doors should remain firmly shut to make sure that Christmas doesn't come all at once. For cats with no willpower, you might need to bring the calendar out for a short time only while she opens the door to collect her treat, and then put it away again for the next day.

THE CANDY MAN

This game was made using an empty chocolate box which has ready-made 'containers' in the inner packaging. Cut little doors above each container and, if you wish, decorate the box because you'll be bringing out this one again and again.

▲ ABOVE Mmm ... Fish Flourish with a Crunchy Coating – my favourite centre!

▼ BELOW Once your cat has got the hang of the game, try hiding treats behind just one or two doors and see how long she takes to home in on the goodies.

Take Me Out to the Ballgame

Who would have thought the humble ping-pong ball could have so many cat-friendly uses? From pinball to football, it is just the right size and weight to be batted about by a small paw. Ball games are good for that all-important paw–eye coordination, building team spirit and for helping hyperactive cats to use up their surplus energy as play can get quite frantic. Some of the commercially available toys include balls, but there are plenty of home-made ball games that you can play too.

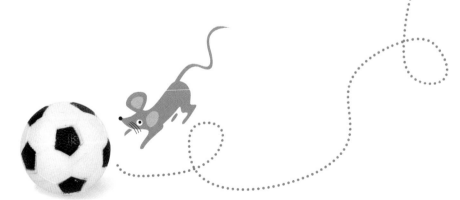

▶ RIGHT Phew! Another penalty saved thanks to a cool head, a strong nerve and lightning reactions.

▲▼ ABOVE AND BELOW Transform a ping-pong ball by drawing on it a soccer ball design in non-toxic ink. It won't improve your cat's ball skills but it will look great in the team photos.

Penalty Shoot Out

As the manager, you can play your game-loving cat in any position – most are very versatile, able to play in attack as well as in defence, and can 'kick' with any paw. Try your cat out in goal first. Position her in front of the goal (or it might be easier to position the goal behind her!) and flick the ball at the goal and see how many 'penalties' she can save. If she lets too many through, or becomes more interested in chasing the ball around the back of the net, check out her ball control skills instead by passing her the ball and allowing her to dribble. You may find she's a born natural.

SLAPSHOT SUPERSTAR

If football doesn't turn out to be your cat's game, try ice hockey instead. Played on a smooth, slippery floor using a small, flat, plastic bottle cap as a puck, the moves will be fast and furious, and watch out for those slapshots – your cat could have major league potential.

▼ BELOW A small plastic or wire basket makes a great goal. If you need to secure it in position, use a few blobs of reusable adhesive tack.

Pinball Wizard

nleash the gaming wizardry in your cat with this low-tech version of the pinball machine. It may be lacking in flashing lights and electronic noises, but it will still provide your cat with plenty of good old-fashioned entertainment. With front paws for flipping and a nose for nudging, your cat will quickly master ball control and earn a replay. It's a great game for cats who are home alone because, once set up safely on a flat surface, you don't need to stay around to put money in a slot or to supervise play. When your cat loses interest and stalks off you'll know it's game over. Then again, it's a great place for a little nap …

▶ RIGHT Having just played 'a mean pinball' this cat is just recharging his batteries before the replay.

▶ RIGHT Strategically positioned cans or cups and pieces of card anchored to the box help to guide the ball around the play area.

THE LOWDOWN

||||||||||||||||||||||||||||||||||||||||||||||||||||||||||||||||||||||||||||||||

All you need for this game is a large container with low sides, one or more ping-pong balls, and several small cylindrical obstacles. You can achieve this by cutting down a large cardboard box, or you might adapt a roomy plant tray or an under-bed storage container, as your machine. Your obstacles can be small unopened cans, or we used colourful plastic cups. The cans should be full and unopened so that they are not easily moved out of place. If you use cups, you may need to use a little adhesive tack on the downturned rims. Position the obstacles at intervals around the container, place one or two ping-pong balls inside, and let the game begin!

◀ LEFT The bigger the better. Climbing into the pinball machine itself may be a little unorthodox, but it makes it easier for your cat to flip and nudge the ball around the play area.

▼ BELOW Paw-sing for thought and considering all the options, this cat is very alert and about to tackle the box from a different angle.

▼ BELOW Cats are very dextrous with their paws. Curving them inwards to form a grip, they can also grip with their claws and can stretch and move their toes separately.

Box of Balls

This one is guaranteed to drive a cat wild – he can look, he can touch, but can he get the balls out of the box? In fact, some of the holes in the box are big enough for the balls to pass through easily but cats love a challenge. When playing with toys on their own, they often make the game more difficult quite deliberately by stalking and pouncing from around a chair or table leg, or by batting their toy into an awkward position. This tantalising game has so many openings for inquisitive, probing paws, your cat just won't know which one to try first. You can refill it with any of his favourite toys.

BOXED IN
IIIIIIIIIIIIIIIIIIIIIIIIIIIIIIIIIIIIIIIIIIIIIIIIIIIIIIIIIIIIIIIIIIIIIIIIIIII

Cut out a series of holes in the sides and along the top of a shallow cardboard box and seal it closed. Reinforce the holes with a border of thinner card, painted, if you wish, with non-toxic paint. The holes should be large enough for your cat to insert a paw easily, but two or three should be slightly larger, wide enough to enable your cat to hook out one of the balls that you place inside.

◀ LEFT First choose your ball …

▼ BELOW … and then hook it with your paw. Make sure some of the holes are large enough for your cat to reach inside with the full length of his front paw.

Junior Accountant

Test your cat's number-crunching abilities with a handy toy abacus. If your cat isn't sure how to play this particular ball game at first, attach a small feather to one of the balls or wedge a treat that has a tantalising scent inside a ball to attract her interest. She will soon put up a curious paw and, once she's got the hang of it, start to pat the balls, making them spin around or whizz up and down the dowelling arms. To add variation to the game suspend a small cat-friendly toy securely from one of the dowelling arms and substitute plastic shower curtain rings for the balls on another.

▲ ABOVE Checking out the new game. The Junior Accountant game will provide plenty of mental stimulation as well as test your cat's dexterity with her paws.

▶ RIGHT Provided there are no small parts that can be pulled off and swallowed, your cat can be left to play this game on her own.

MATHS DEGREE NOT NEEDED

||||||||||||||||||||||||||||||||||||||||||||||||||||||||||||||||||||||||||||||||||||||||||||||||||||||

This abacus is made from an old wooden mug tree
to which several pieces of dowelling were fixed at
right angles. We threaded practice golf balls onto
the dowelling. The balls should be able to move
to left and right freely and be loose enough to spin.
Secure the base with adhesive so that it stays upright.

▲ ABOVE Thread several balls
along each piece of dowelling to
achieve the abacus look and vary
the length of the arms if you wish.

▶ RIGHT Leave the ends free so
that your cat can knock the balls
right off, or create a stop by gluing a
small disk of wood at the end.

SAFETY Make sure that the ends
of the dowelling and
any stops that you glue in place are sanded
so that the edges are round and cannot
harm your cat. Don't use balls that are small
enough to be swallowed if they can be
pulled right off the dowelling arms.

One-Track Mind

This colourful doughnut-shaped toy is guaranteed to grab the attention of most cats. It consists of an enclosed circular track which contains a small ball. The track is just big enough to allow an inquisitive feline paw to reach the ball inside but not to let the ball out. Your cat probably will need little in the way of encouragement to play with this toy and she can be left to play with it on her own quite happily, which makes it an ideal toy to leave out for your cat when she is home alone. However, the design of this game makes it impossible for your cat to get the ball out of the track, so if she shows signs of frustration it is best to place a time limit on play.

▼ BELOW Got it! This cat is using a classic hooking action with her paw to try and retrieve the ball.

◀ ▼ LEFT AND CENTRE
This cat's whiskers with their
sensitive nerve endings have told
her that there is just enough room
in the centre of the doughnut to fit
a small feline face.

▼ BELOW With ears well forward
and whiskers fanned out, this cat is
attentive, alert and fully primed for
some action.

OUTDOOR TRACK

Make your own outdoor track for the
garden using PVC guttering. Lay a couple
of sections on the ground, joining them
together with an angled junction that
changes the track direction. Your cat can
enjoy batting a ball and chasing it up and
down this home-made track.

▲ ABOVE If there are two of you, try a game of piggy-in-the-middle. Throw the ball over your cat's head, gently at first, at an easily accessible height.

Acrobat Cat

Among all their other talents, cats are natural athletes. Their powerful hind quarters can launch them high in the air and their supple bodies enable them to twist and turn in some amazing stunts that would look more at home in the circus than in your living room. Lithe, younger cats are particularly good at leaping about in play and can jump surprisingly high after a favourite toy. From a sitting position some cats can launch themselves so high you would think they were on a trampoline. Throw balls, dangle feathers or swing a toy – you'll soon get your cat leaping around like Olga Korbut.

▲ ABOVE Like dogs, cats walk directly on their toes. Standing upright on the toes of their hind legs it is surprising just how high they can reach.

▲▶ ABOVE AND RIGHT When she gets the idea, she will leap for the ball and try to intercept it. Always make sure that she is able to catch it several times during the game to give her the satisfaction of winning.

SAFETY Cats are extremely cautious, sensible creatures and normally judge distances and movements carefully, but they could overreach themselves in the excitement of a game. Play in a safe place and not too near furniture.

Working Out

Our specially designed workouts will challenge and stimulate your cat both mentally and physically. From gym activities and circuit training to scratching exercises for those all-important paws and claws, we ensure your cat will soon be in fine shape from the ends of his whiskers to the tip of his tail. And there's plenty of scope for helping with those emotional issues, including learning anger management, and relieving day-to-day tension and stress.

Boxerthon

Seconds away, round one. One of your cat's natural actions with his front paws is the batting movement, carried out with the flat of the paw, claws sheathed. In Boxerthon he can bat and swipe at a small 'punch ball' attached to an upright spring or stick in true featherweight style. This game is good for concentration, coordination and for getting rid of any pent-up feelings (cats often use the batting action to chastise fellow felines or humans) – and is great exercise for his upper body, too. He'll soon be floating like a butterfly and stinging like a bee.

▶ RIGHT Once the 'punch ball' is set in motion, your cat will enjoy batting it to start up the action again. You may find two can play at this one.

◀ LEFT Never, ever should you take your eye off the game – even a friendly team-player will take advantage immediately!

ROCKY II

||||||||||||||||||||||||||||||||||||||||||||||||||||||||||||||||||||||||||||||||

Cat-sized punch balls are available to buy commercially. They are normally mounted on a strong spring attached to a suction cup that you can stick onto a flat surface. You can also improvise and make your own by attaching a pliable stick or upright spring to a weighted base, or by using a slightly longer stick with a small lightweight ball attached, placed in a flowerpot, anchored down with either soil or with florist's oasis.

Kit Fitness

After a hard day's snoozing, napping and sleeping, it's good to work up a sweat at the gym. The aim of this version of circuit training is to get your feline friend moving around the room, jumping from one level to another, making him stretch and exercise. He will also be stimulated mentally by having a new arrangement of familiar objects to investigate and having to work out how to tackle some of the gym 'equipment'. If he seems a little reluctant at first, place one or two toys around the course to encourage him.

▲ ABOVE A confident cat needs little persuasion to crawl through an improvised tunnel, as well as jump upon it.

▼ BELOW Superb coordination, balance and an innate urge to explore anything new mean that your cat will soon be up on the circuit.

SAFETY Folding household ladders are not safe for cats, so don't be tempted to use these in your game of different levels.

◀ LEFT Get a grip! The rolled-up rug makes for an easy descent, and offers a chance to get those claws up to scratch too.

▶ RIGHT You'll know when it's game over – your cat will take the quickest way down.

A SPRING IN THEIR STEP

|||||||||||||||||||||||||||||||||||||||||||||||||||||||||||||||||||||||||||||||||||

Powerful hind legs give cats the ability to clear five times their own height. When jumping onto a high fence they use their claws like tiny clamps to dig in and haul themselves up. Watch how carefully your cat judges the distance before he jumps – he will rarely get it wrong.

SAFETY Stay on hand if your cat is older or normally an indoors-only pet – he will almost certainly enjoy an appreciative audience.

▼ LEFT Suspend several toys or a feather from the branches of a shrub or small tree at various heights so he can play seated or sitting.

▲ ABOVE Encourage your cat to move about from one level to another. Set up a plank as a ramp or position a table and a chair next to a wall so he can use each as a 'stepping stone' to the next, making him jump and stretch.

◀ BELOW When this colourful windmill is blown around in the breeze it will attract his attention.

Cat Athlete!

Cats are naturally agile and have excellent balance. You might wince when your cat tiptoes neatly along the top of the narrowest of fences or climbs up a tree for a good view but he is only doing what comes easily and is perfectly happy and safe. If your cat has access to a patio area or garden to call his own, encourage him to play with the ordinary items that you find there. These simple ideas will stimulate and entertain him, as well as help him to stay fit and active.

BUILT FOR BALANCE

A cat has more bones in its body than a human. Its extra-flexible backbone allows it to rotate in mid-air and fall on its feet, arching its back to cushion the landing. A cat's long tail comes in handy to aid its already superb sense of balance. The structure of a cat's collarbone and its narrow chest enables it to walk with ease along the tops of narrow fences, positioning its paws closely together as it walks.

▲ ABOVE Hang toys from a trellis or encourage your cat to weave in and out of it by pulling a piece of string through the gaps.

Mission Impossible

Almost all cats enjoy exploring tunnels, whether they are boisterous toms who enjoy a rough and tumble, or timid females who wouldn't say boo to a little mouse. Tunnels provide adventure and entertainment and pander to your cat's natural need to investigate any and every dark hole available. Specially made fabric tunnels for cats are available in sections that can be used singly or joined together to make a longer tunnel. Rigid tunnels made of plush-covered metal are also available, with holes at intervals along the top so your cat can 'up periscope' to check out the lie of the land mid-tunnel.

▼ BELOW Tunnels are perfect for cats on secret missions and more than one 'agent' can patrol at a time.

▲ ABOVE A cat's ability to see well in dim light means that most are happy to explore dark places that other animals might find scary.

TUNNEL TACTICS

You can easily improvise and make your own tunnel out of large cardboard boxes. Open out both ends and place two or three of the same size end to end to create an instant tunnel that also folds flat when you want it tidied away.

▲ ABOVE Fabric tunnels are useful because they squash down flat for easy storage and have side entrances or junction sections that give cats a choice of route mid-way.

▼ BELOW Always check the tunnel before you put it away, in case your cat has decided to take forty winks mid-tunnel.

▲ ABOVE Some tunnels have toys built in, such as a toy mouse suspended from the ceiling so your cat can play 'Murder in the Dark'. You can also throw a ball into the tunnel for your cat to chase.

Bubble Trouble

Remember your fascination with bubbles as a child? Your cat will enjoy playing with them just as much as you once did. All you need to play Bubble Trouble is some children's bubble soap but you can also make your own (*see Box below*). Blow the bubbles above your cat's head and watch the fun. Blow them high and his excitement will build as he watches them float down. As soon as the bubbles come within reach he will swat at them or pounce on any that settle on the floor. You'll know when it's time to stop if he stalks off in a huff. Some cats find having their 'prey' vanish beneath their paws just a little too frustrating.

▲ ABOVE Although this is not a position your cat will like to hold for long, he can sit on his haunches with tail stretched out at the back for balance and paws raised ready to swipe at the bubbles.

HOME-BREWED BUBBLES

YOU NEED:
$^{1}/_{2}$ cup liquid soap
5 cups distilled or bottled water
2 tablespoons glycerine (or fine sugar)
wire (to make the wand)

Carefully mix the soap, water and glycerine well in a bowl (shaking them in a bottle or jar makes too much foam). Bend the wire into a small, compact circle, leaving enough for a handle. Dip it into the mixture and blow gently.

▶ RIGHT This is a gentle game suitable for all ages – older cats who feel less inclined to move quickly should enjoy it as well as energetic teenagers.

◀ LEFT Your cat will watch as the bubbles descend gently, take aim, then swat at them with a paw. Some commercially made bubble solution is scented with catnip as an added attraction.

Toy Store

Your cat can shop till she drops at this self-service toy store open 24/7. As store manager, your role is to keep the shelves stocked with interesting-looking toys so that she has plenty of choices. Place two or three different toys on each shelf so that she can choose the one she wants to play with. Making her choice from each shelf and checking out what's on special offer this week will be as much part of the game as playing with the toys selected. Add to the shopping trolley and then proceed to the checkout!

▼ BELOW It is a good idea to position the toy store against a wall in case it should get knocked over in the rush at sale time.

◀ LEFT Provided cat-friendly only toys are on offer, the toy store is perfectly safe to leave out when you are not around. Your cat will learn where her toys are kept, though she is unlikely to go so far as to put them away.

SAFETY Make sure your toy store only sells toys that are safe for cats. They should not be small enough to swallow and cause a choking hazard, and string or wool can also be swallowed, causing great harm (*see page 10*).

ONE-STOP STORE

Cut a hole in the lid of a cardboard box measuring around 50 x 30 x 10 millimetres, leaving a 12-millimetre margin around the edge. Reinforce the base with corrugated card. Cut strips of card as shelves and glue them in position, then place the lid on the box. Cut a rectangle of thinner card for an awning, paint it with contrasting stripes and glue in position.

▼ BELOW This one looks fun. Your cat will skilfully select her chosen toy from the shelf with a well-aimed paw.

▲ ABOVE Well-stocked shelves, with a low lip on the bottom shelf to contain balls that might otherwise roll off too easily.

Caticure

Unlike dogs, cats have no need of being packed off to the equivalent of the pooch parlour to be groomed – their small rough tongues provide all the beauty care they need. And when it comes to claw care, cats are just as self-sufficient, provided there is a handy tree trunk or piece of wood to help them keep their claws nicely shaped and buffed. Unfortunately, as far as your cat is concerned, your antique chair leg is just as good, so it is important to provide a suitable and fun alternative that will divert his attention from your treasured items of furniture, especially for the stay-indoors cat.

▲ ABOVE A little catnip sprayed onto the post will tell your cat that this one, unlike your best furniture, is all for him.

▼ BELOW The claws on all four paws can be expertly sharpened if you can position your post to give your cat enough room to stretch out as well as up.

STRETCH AND SCRATCH

Those inner cardboard tubes used by shops to display fabric for making dresses and curtains are very sturdy and come in useful lengths. You can make your cat a dedicated scratching post by winding natural cord or rope tightly around the post. Covering the tube in double-sided adhesive first will help to keep the cord in place, and you will need to secure the ends tightly inside the tube with tape so that those caticured nails cannot pull it loose.

▲ ABOVE Make sure your post is firmly secured to withstand the action of four furry feet.

▲ ABOVE A purchased small scratching mat is useful where space is limited. You may need to position it always in the same spot to encourage your cat to scratch only where it's allowed!

▼ LEFT The holes in the sides of this scratching box double up as a game. Throw a toy or two through the hole for a little après-Scratch 'n Sniff play.

Scratch 'n' Sniff

You can rest easy in the knowledge that your cat is being completely eco-friendly when sharpening her claws on a scratching box made of layers of biodegradable cardboard (and far better here than on your finest furniture or carpet). A good scratching session is also your cat's way of keeping her claws perfectly manicured as the spongy, corrugated cardboard will clean off any dirt as your cat sinks her claws into it. The feel of the warm rough surface beneath your cat's paws is normally enough to have her scratching in the right place immediately, but should any encouragement be required, try sprinkling a little catnip over the surface and she will soon be enjoying the complete Scratch 'n' Sniff experience.

▶ RIGHT Beauty school drop-out? No, simply demonstrating all cats' natural ability to curl up for a quiet nap anywhere.

PRACTICAL & SCRATCHABLE

If the scratching board is removable, when one end becomes worn you can take it out and turn it around so that board is used to the full. Some boards are also reversible and you can usually buy replacement boards to prolong the life of the board support. Cardboard scratchers to hang on a door or mount on a wall are also available.

▼ BELOW Climb every mountain. Cats like to climb and stretch when they are scratching.

▼ BELOW Dangle a toy from the scratching box to attract her attention to it rather than to your furniture or best rug.

MAGIC CARPET

If the mat is small enough – small squares of carpet samples are ideal – pierce a hole in one corner, attach a length of cord and pull your cat on a magic carpet ride around the room. The movement will soon provoke him into another Mat Attack.

▼ BELOW Hey! You looking at me? Mat Attack will help your cat release all his pent-up grrrrr-emotion.

▼ BELOW Another game that makes use of a simple household item, but suitable for old rugs and mats only.

◄ LEFT Exercise caution when playing Mat Attack with your bare hand, though most mats should be thick enough to protect you from those penetrating claws.

▲ ABOVE Encourage him to roll on his side. He will probably grasp the mat with his front paws and then kick it with his back legs – a great tension-relieving exercise.

Mat Attack

This is a great game for feline anger management that avoids group therapy and role play. It enables your cat to get rid of his aggression by attacking a rug or mat and gives him a useful workout too.

If your cat does not attack spontaneously, try sliding a pen or a stick beneath the mat, flip the corner up and down, or jerk the mat when your cat is sitting on it to produce a reaction. He will be unable to resist making a lightning pounce. Or try rolling the mat around him gently and then pulling at one end to unroll him, Cleopatra-style, or try sliding the 'cat roll' about the floor.

Light Fantasy

This game is great fun both for you and your cat. Most cats just love chasing the beam of a torch around a room and it offers you the perfect after-dinner entertainment. You get to relax on the sofa, while your cat does all the physical work, tripping the Light Fantasy.

Use a torch with a thin beam and play it across the floor and up and down the walls of a darkened room. Complete darkness is not required, provided the beam can be seen clearly – just drawing the curtains and dimming the lights should be sufficient. Your cat will go crazy chasing the beam. It is a great way to encourage even the most laid-back of feline couch-potatoes to take some badly needed exercise.

SAFETY Never use a laser light, only a torch. Don't ever shine the beam directly into your cat's eyes. Apart from risking damage to the retina, she won't like it.

▶ RIGHT Contrary to popular belief, cats cannot see in the dark. But in low light they have six times better vision than humans.

NIGHT LIGHT

||||||||||||||||||||||||||||||||||||||||||||||||||||||||||||||||||||||||||||||||||||||||||||||||||||||||||||||

This game really excites most cats and they love chasing after the darting light but the game can get fast and furious pretty quickly. To keep things safe, concentrate on playing the torch beam across the floor and up and down the bottom of walls at no more than cat-accessible height.

▲ ABOVE These light balls are activated by motion and light up in different colours when they are batted around.

▲ ABOVE Try switching the light off and then on again, pointing at a different wall. Your cat may be confounded at first, but not for long.

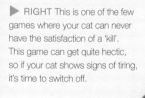

▶ RIGHT This is one of the few games where your cat can never have the satisfaction of a 'kill'. This game can get quite hectic, so if your cat shows signs of tiring, it's time to switch off.

Hide and Seek

Cats operate on a need-to-know basis. They always need to know what is in that bag, box, bowl, behind that chair … you name it, they're nosing in there. So any games that involve first stimulating and then satisfying their all-consuming curiosity are bound to be a hit. Several of these games also fulfil that other feline fixation, the need to hide away out of sight, just in case some small innocent rodent should happen to be passing, or failing that, for a nice long snooze post-play.

Feline Fetch

A wet nose and a panting tongue are not the only qualifications for this game; small purry creatures with short noses, almond eyes and plenty of whiskers can play fetch too. Cat owners might be surprised at the idea of playing a retrieving game but some cats even invent it themselves, bringing a favourite toy for their owners to throw – in which case it's up to you realise what's in his mind. But if your cat hasn't thought of a way of getting you to play with him yet, you can teach him, but only provided he is willing to learn.

◄ LEFT Attract your cat's attention and show him the toy that you wish to throw.

► RIGHT Throw the toy where he can see it land, not too far away. Use your hand to follow through, pointing in the direction of the throw.

▼ BELOW Choose a toy he likes and one that he can pick up easily in his mouth. Don't use a toy filled with catnip, though, as the scent will be too distracting.

A FETCHING HABIT

‖‖

Pick a time when your cat is attentive, take a toy, play with it in front of him, and throw it. If he goes after it, give him a lot of praise and call him to come back to you. If he stays playing with the toy, still praise him but take it from him, return to your position, and throw it again in a different direction. Repeat this several times, and several days in a row. If he gets the idea and likes the game, he'll start bringing his toys to you to throw.

SAFETY If your cat likes retrieving wool, make sure you stay with him, and put the toy away when the game's over.

▼ BELOW Independently minded cats – unlike dogs – only play this game to please themselves not their owners.

It's Alive!

It may not look like much, but beauty is in the eye of the beholder and your cat will just love a plain old grocery bag. Most cats make a beeline for a bag lying on the floor with just a quiet snooze in mind, so turning one into a game is a real bonus.

In this game your cat will think that a small animal is moving around inside the bag. He will be instantly attracted by the movement and will stalk and pounce, trying to capture the moving shape between his paws. The more it moves around the crazier he will get. See how long it takes before he gets through the bottom of the bag!

▲ ABOVE There is a variety of self-powered toys available – from battery-powered and wind-up mice to hamsters and chickens – that wobble across the floor when you pull their string.

▼ BELOW Cats are extremely responsive to movement, so it won't be long before your cat is climbing in the bag after a wobbling chicken!

THE WIND-UP BOOGIE

|||||||||||||||||||||||||||||||||||||||||||||||||||||||||||||||||||||||||||||||||||||||||||||||

All you need is a toy that moves under its own momentum such as a wind-up or battery-powered toy. Wind it up or switch it on and place it inside the bag. Fold over the end of the bag so that the toy cannot escape and your cat cannot see it and let the fun get under way.

▼ BELOW No self-respecting cat will be able to ignore the rodent-style rustling caused by a wind-up mouse trying to escape from a paper bag.

◄ LEFT Heeeere's Johnny! Those gleaming eyes and razor-sharp claws are enough to chase away even the biggest, boldest motovatin' mouse.

▼ BELOW The inevitable result: one tired but victorious cat, one torn paper bag, and one exhausted wind-up toy.

SAFETY Always check the toy for small parts that could come off easily and be swallowed. Only use a paper bag, never plastic, and always cut the handles off first (*see page 10*).

▲ ABOVE Attach a few feathers and toys to the outside of the bag and thread small cat-friendly items through the string, such as a lightweight ball or a plastic shower curtain ring.

Bags of Fun

▼ BELOW A fairly thick bag or a sack made of several layers is best so that the paper won't tear easily when the string is pulled through it.

This is another game involving the humble but infinitely versatile paper bag. Just as most young children are more interested in the packaging than in the toy inside, cats love them. Make this one extra fun by attaching toys to the outside of the bag as well as placing them inside, then your cat can choose to play inside or out and will have plenty to investigate and stimulate his interest. He will also like the crinkly sound that the bag makes when he jumps on it and when the game is over he'll probably settle down for a snooze on top or inside.

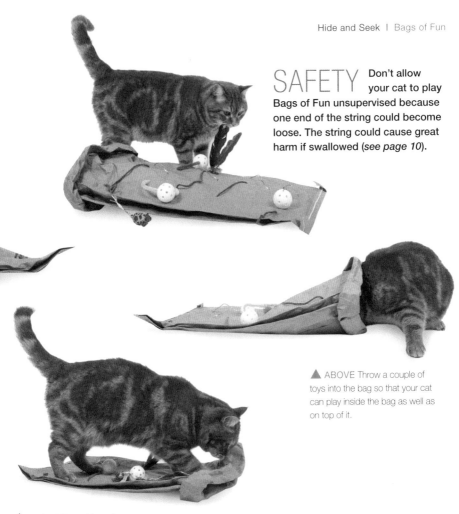

SAFETY Don't allow your cat to play Bags of Fun unsupervised because one end of the string could become loose. The string could cause great harm if swallowed (*see page 10*).

▲ ABOVE Throw a couple of toys into the bag so that your cat can play inside the bag as well as on top of it.

▲ ABOVE Thread the string through fairly loosely so that you can play with your cat by pulling the string through the holes. He will pounce when he sees it moving.

IT'S IN THE BAG

Make a number of holes in one side of the bag and thread string or cord through them. Attach two or three different toys to the string to give your cat plenty to investigate. Make sure that you knot the ends of the string inside the bag securely so that the string cannot be pulled out and the toys remain attached.

Paw Power

Cats have a reputation for loving fish although, paradoxically, also for not being too keen on water – even just stepping in a puddle accidentally will have them shaking their paws in disgust. This game will test just how far your cat will go in pursuit of a little fish action and you may be surprised by the results. He will certainly be interested in watching the fish, just as he likes watching real ones darting about in an aquarium. In this game you will see just how long it takes for his curiosity finally to get the better of him and get his paw wet to hook out that tempting prize.

▲ ABOVE Unless your cat is a Turkish Van (who have been known to enjoy a paddle or even a proper dip in a stream) he is most likely to hook fish that are floating on or near the surface.

► RIGHT Single, brightly colored fish show up well in a clear bowl, though their orange colour almost certainly does not appear so vivid to your cat as it does to you.

▲ ABOVE A high tail means a happy and attentive cat, like this one who has just spotted a nice little fish lurking at the bottom of the bowl.

THE ONE THAT GOT AWAY

For this game you need a goldfish bowl or a similar container part-filled with water. If you use a hollow plastic fish, it will float or, if you expel all the air, it can be made to sink. To make one appear to 'swim' part way up, attach one end of a short length of string to the fish and the other to a small stone. Place the stone in the bottom of the bowl to anchor the fish at the required height.

▲ ABOVE He couldn't possibly get any closer without getting his nose wet! This cat is selecting his fish, just as they do in all the best restaurants – though he doesn't exactly have so much choice.

Crinkle Hat

There's not really a magician's rabbit in this top hat but it's a perfect fit for a cat. It has a great crinkle lining that makes some intriguing rustling sounds when your cat moves around inside it – he might even start looking for some scurrying mice.

Place a small toy or soft ball inside the crinkle hat for him to play with before he snuggles down for a quiet snooze. You won't need to wave your magic wand, he'll jump right in and Hey Presto … your cat is in a hat!

▲ ABOVE Fabric crinkle hats are available commercially but if you make your own you can tailor it as large or small as you please. Uncle Sam-size hats are perfect for snoozing and sitting in, especially if weighted down with a soft cushion.

A HAT FOR A CAT

Use corrugated card to form the crown, taped to a size to accommodate your cat. Cut a circle in thin card to make a brim, and cut out the centre to match the diameter of the crown. Tape the brim all the way around the hat. Use scrunched-up sheets of craft paper to cover the hat, inside and out. Line the inside with more craft paper to add to the crinkle sound. Decorate the hat any way you like.

▲ ABOVE As with anything new in your cat's life, he has to check it out thoroughly by smell first.

▲ ABOVE Having passed the smell test, the next and inevitable stage is to satisfy his curiosity and climb inside.

◀ LEFT Do you think it's a bit big for me? Dangle toys from the rim or tip the hat on its side and throw in a toy so your cat can explore from a different angle.

Chez Miaow

To your highly territorial cat, having a place to call her own is very important – and when it comes to finding the snuggest, cosiest place to practise that most famous of sleep styles, the 'cat nap', your cat knows where it's at. From a cool 'catcienda' to a pent-house suite, the games in this chapter will help your home-loving cat find the perfect des res. And once installed, she can even pull up a basket and watch a DVD for a quiet evening in.

Cool Catcienda

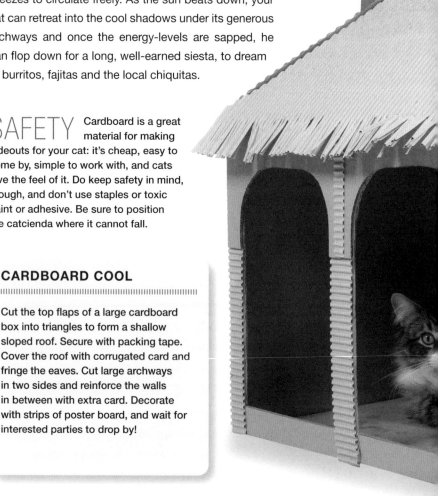

Fiery, hot-blooded cats can keep cool in a catcienda even on sunny days. It can be used both indoors and out, but is ideal for a safely enclosed garden where it offers a shaded place to play while allowing gentle breezes to circulate freely. As the sun beats down, your cat can retreat into the cool shadows under its generous archways and once the energy-levels are sapped, he can flop down for a long, well-earned siesta, to dream of burritos, fajitas and the local chiquitas.

SAFETY

Cardboard is a great material for making hideouts for your cat: it's cheap, easy to come by, simple to work with, and cats love the feel of it. Do keep safety in mind, though, and don't use staples or toxic paint or adhesive. Be sure to position the catcienda where it cannot fall.

CARDBOARD COOL

Cut the top flaps of a large cardboard box into triangles to form a shallow sloped roof. Secure with packing tape. Cover the roof with corrugated card and fringe the eaves. Cut large archways in two sides and reinforce the walls in between with extra card. Decorate with strips of poster board, and wait for interested parties to drop by!

▲ ABOVE Private – Trespassers will be Prosecuted. By rubbing his cheek along the walls, this cat is leaving his scent and making sure other cats know that this is his private property.

◀ LEFT A Cool Catcienda is a great place to spruce up. Cats spend around 30 per cent of their waking hours grooming. They wash more often in hot weather as the evaporation of saliva helps to cool them down.

Cat Condo

Sheets of cardboard and a simple shelving unit translate into one comfortable feline residence – the purrfect property for the urban cat, providing a room with a view or two, a roof terrace for lazy lounging and some interesting nooks and crannies to investigate. And who needs a lift when you have super-springy hind quarters? Ideal for cats who like high-rise living, there's plenty of room to entertain furry friends with no danger of overcrowding in this desirable residence. Viewing essential.

▲ ABOVE Be creative with the front window shapes, but make sure the end windows are large enough for your cat to jump through.

SAFETY A condo must be secure, solid and stable enough to withstand cats leaping in through the windows or directly onto the roof. Screw it to a wall if you don't mind having it as a permanent fixture in your home.

CONDO CONVERSION

A four-shelf wooden bookcase with open sides is the base. Cut two panels out of strong cardboard to fit each end of the bookcase and cut three cat-size access windows in each. Cut three panels of cardboard to fit the front and back of the bookcase and cut one window for each 'floor' in the front panels. Drill small holes in the bookcase and screw the panels into place.

◀ LEFT Honey, I'm home. Checking it out on tiptoe, this cat is about to head straight for the second floor for a nap.

▶ RIGHT If the condo is free-standing, place toys on the ground floor only to make sure it does not topple over in boisterous play. Add carpet and cushions for snug snoozing.

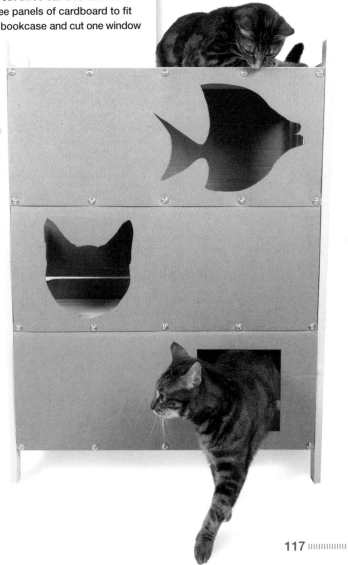

King of the Castle

Cats love to be high up looking down on things. It helps them to feel safe while satisfying their all-important need to know what is going on all around. This game provides plenty of stretching and jumping exercise, helping indoors cats to keep active. You can make a castle out of any cat-friendly items around the house. Elderly or obese cats might need a helping hand to reach the top level of the castle in the form of a conveniently placed chair or stool.

▼ BELOW Make sure that your castle is safe. The top level or levels should be stable and secure enough to withstand the weight of your cat climbing or leaping directly onto it.

TOP CAT

‖‖‖

Social hierarchy is not as pronounced among cats as in many other species, though in multi-cat households one cat becomes top thanks to its strength or mental aptitude. Cats are not such sociable creatures as dogs and are not pack animals – they don't need to belong to a group for security. Having their own territory is all important. Preferring to avoid confrontation, they are less likely to fight to establish dominance than to defend their territory.

◀ LEFT Height is a distinct advantage when your cat wants to establish who's who in the pecking order.

▲ ABOVE What goes up ... cats often opt for the quickest way down.

Country Retreat

With perches, scratching posts and small secure spaces to explore and snooze in, cat trees offer versatile, all-in-one 24-hour entertainment.

There's plenty of opportunity for playful exercise, stretching, scratching, jumping from one level to another, and swiping at a tantalising dangly toy on the way.

And, since all cats love to watch the world go by, if you position the tree near a window, your cat will soon be twitching the curtains in his role as nosy neighbour. It's a pity you don't speak your cat's tongue, or you would soon be hearing all about the comings and goings in your neighbourhood.

▲ ABOVE Sisal-covered posts provide good grip for clambering about the perch and double up as useful scratching posts for cats who like their beauty treatment at home.

▶ RIGHT All those inviting dark caves, hollows and comfy perches are perfect for cat-napping which is good since cats spend two-thirds of their lives sleeping.

RETREAT REQUIREMENTS

The most important requirement for a cat tree is that it is strong, stable and able to withstand a furry bundle leaping onto any part of it at speed. Most are covered with fabric or carpet. If you use sisal make sure it is unoiled (most will be) as oiled sisal is toxic.

▲ ABOVE Hide some treats or a cat-friendly toy or two for your cat to find when exploring a cat tree's nooks and crannies.

◀ LEFT Two or even three can certainly play this game. There is ample room on a large cat tree for more than one cat.

BOXED IN

||||||||||||||||||||||||||||||||||||||||||||||||||||||||||||||||||||||||||||||||||||||||||||||||||||

For an average-size cat, cut a 20 x 20-centimetre arch in one end of a cardboard box and two 10 x 10-centimetre windows in one side. Cut wooden skewers to size and push them down inside the corrugations on the lower window edges and up into the top edges. Glue a 2.5-centimetre-wide cardboard border around each window. As a final touch, add a 'Wanted' poster of your cat's face!

▼ BELOW It may look like a tight fit, but most cats like to squeeze themselves into the smallest of spaces: it helps them to feel secure.

▼ BELOW There's no need for cuffs or a ball and chain: this cat's going quietly.

Escape to Alcatraz

Since all cats like nothing better than holing up somewhere small and cat-sized and love to fit themselves into the snuggest of places, they won't mind doing time in this jail cell.

Place a toy inside the cell to keep your cat from going stir crazy while in solitary and, when it's visiting time, feline felons will get a lot more fun if you poke a feather through the bars rather than a file. In fact, they'll like this jail so much that they'll be tunnelling in instead of tunnelling out.

▼ BELOW He may be entering a maximum security facility but this cat's upright tail shows that he is quite happy and in an alert, investigative mood.

▼ BELOW If your cat is going directly to jail, you can make it more interesting still by providing access via a tunnel. Improvise one with a cardboard box open at both ends placed against the 'cell' entrance.

Couch Cats

Few cats will lift their heads up from the sofa to watch your favourite film, although many will twitch an ear when they hear the Miaow of a fellow feline on the small screen. Most, however, will be unable to resist watching specially recorded cat-interest DVDs. Their attention is caught by movement on screen, so why not use your camcorder to make your cat his personal selection of DVDs featuring scenes of cat-interest wildlife in action – birds, fish, insects and small rodents in the act of flying, swimming, and scurrying across the screen. The perfect TV dinner for your pet!

▲ ABOVE Cats don't mind watching the same film over and over, so you won't need to stock your shelves with a vast library of wildlife DVDs or visit the video shop.

▼ BELOW Some cats respond very quickly, while others need to be shown a DVD several times before they get the idea, or might even try to peer around the back of the screen to see what is going on.

SOUND EFFECTS

Cats are attracted by sound as well as by movement when they hunt, so cat DVDs can also feature bird-calls and scurrying and rustling sounds. There is often little change to the background as it is the movement of the creatures across the screen that interests them. Specially recorded DVDs are shot with a filter that enhances the colours and tones that cats see best.

▼ BELOW Most cats will want to get close to the screen, especially if they like to get interactive.

◄ LEFT Don't be offended if your cat stops for a yawn and a wash after just ten minutes of your home-shot DVD. Cats have a pretty short attention span.

Index

Acknowledgements

The author would like to thank the following people for their very valuable contributions in the creation of this book: Emma Frith, Elise Gaignet and Alison Jenkins for making the wonderful props for the games, despite the often vague instructions, and for interpreting the author's sometimes rather bizarre ideas so skilfully; Lynn Bassett, Joanna Clinch, Stephanie Evans, Holly Johnson and Dawn Martin for allowing us to turn their homes into studios; Sophie Collins for her sane and sound advice; Stephanie Evans for her well-judged contributions, patience and for being such a delight to work with; and Jane Moseley for her Paw Power game, terrific titles and eternal support. Especial thanks to Nick Ridley for his skill with the camera and unfailing ability to capture that perfect pounce.

Thanks also to the real stars of the book – the cats – without whom none of this would have been possible, and who performed selflessly (and admittedly sometimes also for treats) in the face of distracting lights, camera and crew:

| Alfie | Alice | Ant | Beau | Dec | Hatty |

| Jeremy | Louie | Molly | Puzzle | Street Bob |

Finally, thanks to Sandy, the author's much-loved first cat, who introduced her to the world of felines, and Ginger, who adores prawns, country walks and, of course, playing games.